This book belongs to:

____

Date:

____

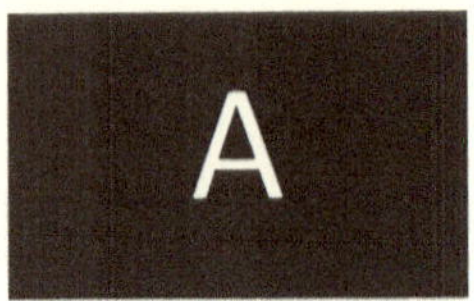

Website:

Username: Email:

Password:

Security Question 1:

Security Answer 1:

Security Question 2:

Security Answer 2:

Notes:

Website:

Username: Email:

Password:

Security Question 1:

Security Answer 1:

Security Question 2:

Security Answer 2:

Notes:

Website:

Username: Email:

Password:

Security Question 1:

Security Answer 1:

Security Question 2:

Security Answer 2:

Notes:

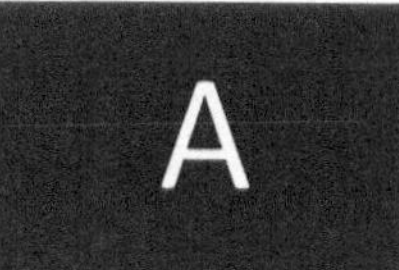

Website:

Username: ___________________ Email: ___________________

Password: ___________________

Security Question 1: ___________________

Security Answer 1: ___________________

Security Question 2: ___________________

Security Answer 2: ___________________

Notes: ___________________

Website:

Username: ___________________ Email: ___________________

Password: ___________________

Security Question 1: ___________________

Security Answer 1: ___________________

Security Question 2: ___________________

Security Answer 2: ___________________

Notes: ___________________

Website:

Username: ___________________ Email: ___________________

Password: ___________________

Security Question 1: ___________________

Security Answer 1: ___________________

Security Question 2: ___________________

Security Answer 2: ___________________

Notes: ___________________

Website:

Username: Email:

Password:

Security Question 1:

Security Answer 1:

Security Question 2:

Security Answer 2:

Notes:

Website:

Username: Email:

Password:

Security Question 1:

Security Answer 1:

Security Question 2:

Security Answer 2:

Notes:

Website:

Username: Email:

Password:

Security Question 1:

Security Answer 1:

Security Question 2:

Security Answer 2:

Notes:

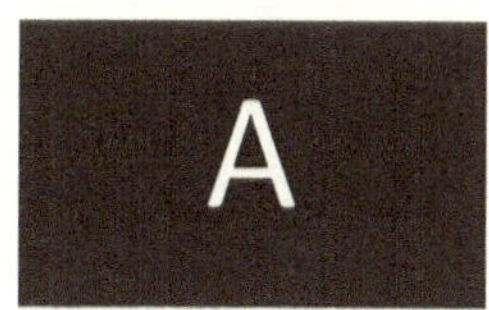

Website:

Username: Email:

Password:

Security Question 1:

Security Answer 1:

Security Question 2:

Security Answer 2:

Notes:

Website:

Username: Email:

Password:

Security Question 1:

Security Answer 1:

Security Question 2:

Security Answer 2:

Notes:

Website:

Username: Email:

Password:

Security Question 1:

Security Answer 1:

Security Question 2:

Security Answer 2:

Notes:

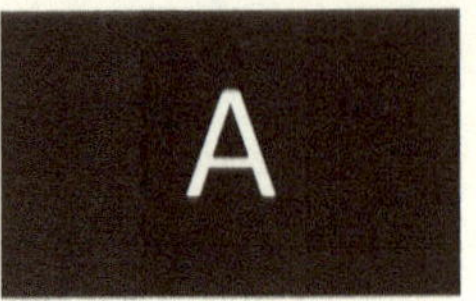

Website:

Username: Email:

Password:

Security Question 1:

Security Answer 1:

Security Question 2:

Security Answer 2:

Notes:

Website:

Username: Email:

Password:

Security Question 1:

Security Answer 1:

Security Question 2:

Security Answer 2:

Notes:

Website:

Username: Email:

Password:

Security Question 1:

Security Answer 1:

Security Question 2:

Security Answer 2:

Notes:

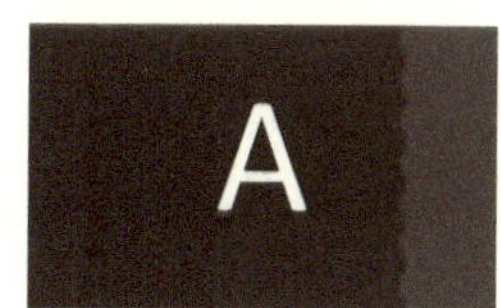

Website:

Username: Email:

Password:

Security Question 1:

Security Answer 1:

Security Question 2:

Security Answer 2:

Notes:

Website:

Username: Email:

Password:

Security Question 1:

Security Answer 1:

Security Question 2:

Security Answer 2:

Notes:

Website:

Username: Email:

Password:

Security Question 1:

Security Answer 1:

Security Question 2:

Security Answer 2:

Notes:

Website:

Username: Email:

Password:

Security Question 1:

Security Answer 1:

Security Question 2:

Security Answer 2:

Notes:

Website:

Username: Email:

Password:

Security Question 1:

Security Answer 1:

Security Question 2:

Security Answer 2:

Notes:

Website:

Username: Email:

Password:

Security Question 1:

Security Answer 1:

Security Question 2:

Security Answer 2:

Notes:

B

Website:

Username: Email:

Password:

Security Question 1:

Security Answer 1:

Security Question 2:

Security Answer 2:

Notes:

Website:

Username: Email:

Password:

Security Question 1:

Security Answer 1:

Security Question 2:

Security Answer 2:

Notes:

Website:

Username: Email:

Password:

Security Question 1:

Security Answer 1:

Security Question 2:

Security Answer 2:

Notes:

B

Website:

Username: Email:

Password:

Security Question 1:

Security Answer 1:

Security Question 2:

Security Answer 2:

Notes:

Website:

Username: Email:

Password:

Security Question 1:

Security Answer 1:

Security Question 2:

Security Answer 2:

Notes:

Website:

Username: Email:

Password:

Security Question 1:

Security Answer 1:

Security Question 2:

Security Answer 2:

Notes:

B

Website:

Username: Email:

Password:

Security Question 1:

Security Answer 1:

Security Question 2:

Security Answer 2:

Notes:

Website:

Username: Email:

Password:

Security Question 1:

Security Answer 1:

Security Question 2:

Security Answer 2:

Notes:

Website:

Username: Email:

Password:

Security Question 1:

Security Answer 1:

Security Question 2:

Security Answer 2:

Notes:

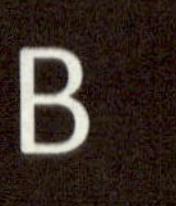

Website:

Username: Email:

Password:

Security Question 1:

Security Answer 1:

Security Question 2:

Security Answer 2:

Notes:

Website:

Username: Email:

Password:

Security Question 1:

Security Answer 1:

Security Question 2:

Security Answer 2:

Notes:

Website:

Username: Email:

Password:

Security Question 1:

Security Answer 1:

Security Question 2:

Security Answer 2:

Notes:

Website:

Username: Email:

Password:

Security Question 1:

Security Answer 1:

Security Question 2:

Security Answer 2:

Notes:

Website:

Username: Email:

Password:

Security Question 1:

Security Answer 1:

Security Question 2:

Security Answer 2:

Notes:

Website:

Username: Email:

Password:

Security Question 1:

Security Answer 1:

Security Question 2:

Security Answer 2:

Notes:

Website:

Username: Email:

Password:

Security Question 1:

Security Answer 1:

Security Question 2:

Security Answer 2:

Notes:

Website:

Username: Email:

Password:

Security Question 1:

Security Answer 1:

Security Question 2:

Security Answer 2:

Notes:

Website:

Username: Email:

Password:

Security Question 1:

Security Answer 1:

Security Question 2:

Security Answer 2:

Notes:

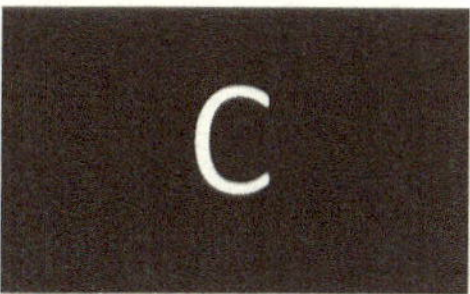

Website:

Username: | Email:

Password:

Security Question 1:

Security Answer 1:

Security Question 2:

Security Answer 2:

Notes:

Website:

Username: | Email:

Password:

Security Question 1:

Security Answer 1:

Security Question 2:

Security Answer 2:

Notes:

Website:

Username: | Email:

Password:

Security Question 1:

Security Answer 1:

Security Question 2:

Security Answer 2:

Notes:

C

Website:

Username:	Email:

Password:

Security Question 1:

Security Answer 1:

Security Question 2:

Security Answer 2:

Notes:

Website:

Username:	Email:

Password:

Security Question 1:

Security Answer 1:

Security Question 2:

Security Answer 2:

Notes:

Website:

Username:	Email:

Password:

Security Question 1:

Security Answer 1:

Security Question 2:

Security Answer 2:

Notes:

Website:

Username: Email:

Password:

Security Question 1:

Security Answer 1:

Security Question 2:

Security Answer 2:

Notes:

Website:

Username: Email:

Password:

Security Question 1:

Security Answer 1:

Security Question 2:

Security Answer 2:

Notes:

Website:

Username: Email:

Password:

Security Question 1:

Security Answer 1:

Security Question 2:

Security Answer 2:

Notes:

Website:

Username: Email:

Password:

Security Question 1:

Security Answer 1:

Security Question 2:

Security Answer 2:

Notes:

Website:

Username: Email:

Password:

Security Question 1:

Security Answer 1:

Security Question 2:

Security Answer 2:

Notes:

Website:

Username: Email:

Password:

Security Question 1:

Security Answer 1:

Security Question 2:

Security Answer 2:

Notes:

C

Website:

Username:	Email:

Password:

Security Question 1:

Security Answer 1:

Security Question 2:

Security Answer 2:

Notes:

Website:

Username:	Email:

Password:

Security Question 1:

Security Answer 1:

Security Question 2:

Security Answer 2:

Notes:

Website:

Username:	Email:

Password:

Security Question 1:

Security Answer 1:

Security Question 2:

Security Answer 2:

Notes:

Website:

Username: Email:

Password:

Security Question 1:

Security Answer 1:

Security Question 2:

Security Answer 2:

Notes:

Website:

Username: Email:

Password:

Security Question 1:

Security Answer 1:

Security Question 2:

Security Answer 2:

Notes:

Website:

Username: Email:

Password:

Security Question 1:

Security Answer 1:

Security Question 2:

Security Answer 2:

Notes:

Website:

Username: Email:

Password:

Security Question 1:

Security Answer 1:

Security Question 2:

Security Answer 2:

Notes:

Website:

Username: Email:

Password:

Security Question 1:

Security Answer 1:

Security Question 2:

Security Answer 2:

Notes:

Website:

Username: Email:

Password:

Security Question 1:

Security Answer 1:

Security Question 2:

Security Answer 2:

Notes:

Website:

Username: Email:

Password:

Security Question 1:

Security Answer 1:

Security Question 2:

Security Answer 2:

Notes:

Website:

Username: Email:

Password:

Security Question 1:

Security Answer 1:

Security Question 2:

Security Answer 2:

Notes:

Website:

Username: Email:

Password:

Security Question 1:

Security Answer 1:

Security Question 2:

Security Answer 2:

Notes:

Website:

Username: Email:

Password:

Security Question 1:

Security Answer 1:

Security Question 2:

Security Answer 2:

Notes:

Website:

Username: Email:

Password:

Security Question 1:

Security Answer 1:

Security Question 2:

Security Answer 2:

Notes:

Website:

Username: Email:

Password:

Security Question 1:

Security Answer 1:

Security Question 2:

Security Answer 2:

Notes:

Website:

Username: Email:

Password:

Security Question 1:

Security Answer 1:

Security Question 2:

Security Answer 2:

Notes:

Website:

Username: Email:

Password:

Security Question 1:

Security Answer 1:

Security Question 2:

Security Answer 2:

Notes:

Website:

Username: Email:

Password:

Security Question 1:

Security Answer 1:

Security Question 2:

Security Answer 2:

Notes:

Website:

Username: ___________________ Email: ___________________

Password: ___________________

Security Question 1: ___________________

Security Answer 1: ___________________

Security Question 2: ___________________

Security Answer 2: ___________________

Notes: ___________________

Website:

Username: ___________________ Email: ___________________

Password: ___________________

Security Question 1: ___________________

Security Answer 1: ___________________

Security Question 2: ___________________

Security Answer 2: ___________________

Notes: ___________________

Website:

Username: ___________________ Email: ___________________

Password: ___________________

Security Question 1: ___________________

Security Answer 1: ___________________

Security Question 2: ___________________

Security Answer 2: ___________________

Notes: ___________________

Website:

Username: Email:

Password:

Security Question 1:

Security Answer 1:

Security Question 2:

Security Answer 2:

Notes:

Website:

Username: Email:

Password:

Security Question 1:

Security Answer 1:

Security Question 2:

Security Answer 2:

Notes:

Website:

Username: Email:

Password:

Security Question 1:

Security Answer 1:

Security Question 2:

Security Answer 2:

Notes:

E

Website:

Username: Email:

Password:

Security Question 1:

Security Answer 1:

Security Question 2:

Security Answer 2:

Notes:

Website:

Username: Email:

Password:

Security Question 1:

Security Answer 1:

Security Question 2:

Security Answer 2:

Notes:

Website:

Username: Email:

Password:

Security Question 1:

Security Answer 1:

Security Question 2:

Security Answer 2:

Notes:

Website:

Username: Email:

Password:

Security Question 1:

Security Answer 1:

Security Question 2:

Security Answer 2:

Notes:

Website:

Username: Email:

Password:

Security Question 1:

Security Answer 1:

Security Question 2:

Security Answer 2:

Notes:

Website:

Username: Email:

Password:

Security Question 1:

Security Answer 1:

Security Question 2:

Security Answer 2:

Notes:

E

Website:

Username: ___________________ Email: ___________________

Password: ___________________

Security Question 1: ___________________

Security Answer 1: ___________________

Security Question 2: ___________________

Security Answer 2: ___________________

Notes: ___________________

Website:

Username: ___________________ Email: ___________________

Password: ___________________

Security Question 1: ___________________

Security Answer 1: ___________________

Security Question 2: ___________________

Security Answer 2: ___________________

Notes: ___________________

Website:

Username: ___________________ Email: ___________________

Password: ___________________

Security Question 1: ___________________

Security Answer 1: ___________________

Security Question 2: ___________________

Security Answer 2: ___________________

Notes: ___________________

Website:

Username: Email:

Password:

Security Question 1:

Security Answer 1:

Security Question 2:

Security Answer 2:

Notes:

Website:

Username: Email:

Password:

Security Question 1:

Security Answer 1:

Security Question 2:

Security Answer 2:

Notes:

Website:

Username: Email:

Password:

Security Question 1:

Security Answer 1:

Security Question 2:

Security Answer 2:

Notes:

E

Website:

Username: Email:

Password:

Security Question 1:

Security Answer 1:

Security Question 2:

Security Answer 2:

Notes:

Website:

Username: Email:

Password:

Security Question 1:

Security Answer 1:

Security Question 2:

Security Answer 2:

Notes:

Website:

Username: Email:

Password:

Security Question 1:

Security Answer 1:

Security Question 2:

Security Answer 2:

Notes:

Website:

Username: **Email:**

Password:

Security Question 1:

Security Answer 1:

Security Question 2:

Security Answer 2:

Notes:

Website:

Username: **Email:**

Password:

Security Question 1:

Security Answer 1:

Security Question 2:

Security Answer 2:

Notes:

Website:

Username: **Email:**

Password:

Security Question 1:

Security Answer 1:

Security Question 2:

Security Answer 2:

Notes:

Website:

Username: Email:

Password:

Security Question 1:

Security Answer 1:

Security Question 2:

Security Answer 2:

Notes:

Website:

Username: Email:

Password:

Security Question 1:

Security Answer 1:

Security Question 2:

Security Answer 2:

Notes:

Website:

Username: Email:

Password:

Security Question 1:

Security Answer 1:

Security Question 2:

Security Answer 2:

Notes:

Website:

Username: Email:

Password:

Security Question 1:

Security Answer 1:

Security Question 2:

Security Answer 2:

Notes:

Website:

Username: Email:

Password:

Security Question 1:

Security Answer 1:

Security Question 2:

Security Answer 2:

Notes:

Website:

Username: Email:

Password:

Security Question 1:

Security Answer 1:

Security Question 2:

Security Answer 2:

Notes:

F

Website:

Username: Email:

Password:

Security Question 1:

Security Answer 1:

Security Question 2:

Security Answer 2:

Notes:

Website:

Username: Email:

Password:

Security Question 1:

Security Answer 1:

Security Question 2:

Security Answer 2:

Notes:

Website:

Username: Email:

Password:

Security Question 1:

Security Answer 1:

Security Question 2:

Security Answer 2:

Notes:

Website:

Username: Email:

Password:

Security Question 1:

Security Answer 1:

Security Question 2:

Security Answer 2:

Notes:

Website:

Username: Email:

Password:

Security Question 1:

Security Answer 1:

Security Question 2:

Security Answer 2:

Notes:

Website:

Username: Email:

Password:

Security Question 1:

Security Answer 1:

Security Question 2:

Security Answer 2:

Notes:

Website:

Username: Email:

Password:

Security Question 1:

Security Answer 1:

Security Question 2:

Security Answer 2:

Notes:

Website:

Username: Email:

Password:

Security Question 1:

Security Answer 1:

Security Question 2:

Security Answer 2:

Notes:

Website:

Username: Email:

Password:

Security Question 1:

Security Answer 1:

Security Question 2:

Security Answer 2:

Notes:

Website:

Username: Email:

Password:

Security Question 1:

Security Answer 1:

Security Question 2:

Security Answer 2:

Notes:

Website:

Username: Email:

Password:

Security Question 1:

Security Answer 1:

Security Question 2:

Security Answer 2:

Notes:

Website:

Username: Email:

Password:

Security Question 1:

Security Answer 1:

Security Question 2:

Security Answer 2:

Notes:

G

Website:

Username: Email:

Password:

Security Question 1:

Security Answer 1:

Security Question 2:

Security Answer 2:

Notes:

Website:

Username: Email:

Password:

Security Question 1:

Security Answer 1:

Security Question 2:

Security Answer 2:

Notes:

Website:

Username: Email:

Password:

Security Question 1:

Security Answer 1:

Security Question 2:

Security Answer 2:

Notes:

Website:

Username: Email:

Password:

Security Question 1:

Security Answer 1:

Security Question 2:

Security Answer 2:

Notes:

Website:

Username: Email:

Password:

Security Question 1:

Security Answer 1:

Security Question 2:

Security Answer 2:

Notes:

Website:

Username: Email:

Password:

Security Question 1:

Security Answer 1:

Security Question 2:

Security Answer 2:

Notes:

G

Website:

Username: Email:

Password:

Security Question 1:

Security Answer 1:

Security Question 2:

Security Answer 2:

Notes:

Website:

Username: Email:

Password:

Security Question 1:

Security Answer 1:

Security Question 2:

Security Answer 2:

Notes:

Website:

Username: Email:

Password:

Security Question 1:

Security Answer 1:

Security Question 2:

Security Answer 2:

Notes:

G

Website:

Username: Email:

Password:

Security Question 1:

Security Answer 1:

Security Question 2:

Security Answer 2:

Notes:

Website:

Username: Email:

Password:

Security Question 1:

Security Answer 1:

Security Question 2:

Security Answer 2:

Notes:

Website:

Username: Email:

Password:

Security Question 1:

Security Answer 1:

Security Question 2:

Security Answer 2:

Notes:

Website:

Username: Email:

Password:

Security Question 1:

Security Answer 1:

Security Question 2:

Security Answer 2:

Notes:

Website:

Username: Email:

Password:

Security Question 1:

Security Answer 1:

Security Question 2:

Security Answer 2:

Notes:

Website:

Username: Email:

Password:

Security Question 1:

Security Answer 1:

Security Question 2:

Security Answer 2:

Notes:

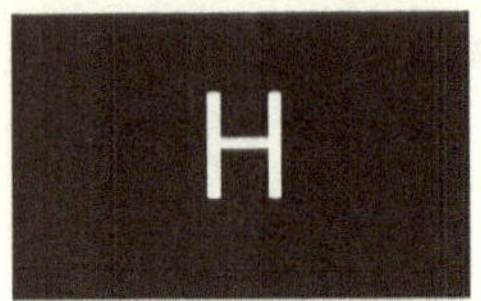

Website:

Username: Email:

Password:

Security Question 1:

Security Answer 1:

Security Question 2:

Security Answer 2:

Notes:

Website:

Username: Email:

Password:

Security Question 1:

Security Answer 1:

Security Question 2:

Security Answer 2:

Notes:

Website:

Username: Email:

Password:

Security Question 1:

Security Answer 1:

Security Question 2:

Security Answer 2:

Notes:

Website:

Username: Email:

Password:

Security Question 1:

Security Answer 1:

Security Question 2:

Security Answer 2:

Notes:

Website:

Username: Email:

Password:

Security Question 1:

Security Answer 1:

Security Question 2:

Security Answer 2:

Notes:

Website:

Username: Email:

Password:

Security Question 1:

Security Answer 1:

Security Question 2:

Security Answer 2:

Notes:

Website:

Username: Email:

Password:

Security Question 1:

Security Answer 1:

Security Question 2:

Security Answer 2:

Notes:

Website:

Username: Email:

Password:

Security Question 1:

Security Answer 1:

Security Question 2:

Security Answer 2:

Notes:

Website:

Username: Email:

Password:

Security Question 1:

Security Answer 1:

Security Question 2:

Security Answer 2:

Notes:

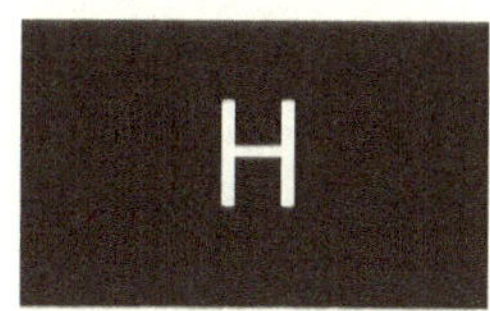

Website:

Username: Email:

Password:

Security Question 1:

Security Answer 1:

Security Question 2:

Security Answer 2:

Notes:

Website:

Username: Email:

Password:

Security Question 1:

Security Answer 1:

Security Question 2:

Security Answer 2:

Notes:

Website:

Username: Email:

Password:

Security Question 1:

Security Answer 1:

Security Question 2:

Security Answer 2:

Notes:

Website:

Username: Email:

Password:

Security Question 1:

Security Answer 1:

Security Question 2:

Security Answer 2:

Notes:

Website:

Username: Email:

Password:

Security Question 1:

Security Answer 1:

Security Question 2:

Security Answer 2:

Notes:

Website:

Username: Email:

Password:

Security Question 1:

Security Answer 1:

Security Question 2:

Security Answer 2:

Notes:

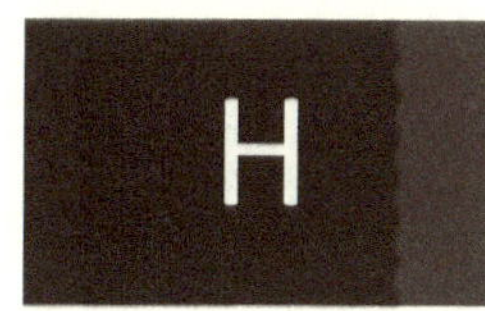

Website:

Username: Email:

Password:

Security Question 1:

Security Answer 1:

Security Question 2:

Security Answer 2:

Notes:

Website:

Username: Email:

Password:

Security Question 1:

Security Answer 1:

Security Question 2:

Security Answer 2:

Notes:

Website:

Username: Email:

Password:

Security Question 1:

Security Answer 1:

Security Question 2:

Security Answer 2:

Notes:

Website:

Username: ___________________ Email: ___________________

Password: ___________________

Security Question 1: ___________________

Security Answer 1: ___________________

Security Question 2: ___________________

Security Answer 2: ___________________

Notes: ___________________

Website:

Username: ___________________ Email: ___________________

Password: ___________________

Security Question 1: ___________________

Security Answer 1: ___________________

Security Question 2: ___________________

Security Answer 2: ___________________

Notes: ___________________

Website:

Username: ___________________ Email: ___________________

Password: ___________________

Security Question 1: ___________________

Security Answer 1: ___________________

Security Question 2: ___________________

Security Answer 2: ___________________

Notes: ___________________

Website:

Username: _______________ Email: _______________

Password:

Security Question 1:

Security Answer 1:

Security Question 2:

Security Answer 2:

Notes:

Website:

Username: _______________ Email: _______________

Password:

Security Question 1:

Security Answer 1:

Security Question 2:

Security Answer 2:

Notes:

Website:

Username: _______________ Email: _______________

Password:

Security Question 1:

Security Answer 1:

Security Question 2:

Security Answer 2:

Notes:

Website:

Username: Email:

Password:

Security Question 1:

Security Answer 1:

Security Question 2:

Security Answer 2:

Notes:

Website:

Username: Email:

Password:

Security Question 1:

Security Answer 1:

Security Question 2:

Security Answer 2:

Notes:

Website:

Username: Email:

Password:

Security Question 1:

Security Answer 1:

Security Question 2:

Security Answer 2:

Notes:

Username: Email:

Password:

Security Question 1:

Security Answer 1:

Security Question 2:

Security Answer 2:

Notes:

Website:

Username: Email:

Password:

Security Question 1:

Security Answer 1:

Security Question 2:

Security Answer 2:

Notes:

Website:

Username: Email:

Password:

Security Question 1:

Security Answer 1:

Security Question 2:

Security Answer 2:

Notes:

Website:

Username: Email:

Password:

Security Question 1:

Security Answer 1:

Security Question 2:

Security Answer 2:

Notes:

Website:

Username: Email:

Password:

Security Question 1:

Security Answer 1:

Security Question 2:

Security Answer 2:

Notes:

Website:

Username: Email:

Password:

Security Question 1:

Security Answer 1:

Security Question 2:

Security Answer 2:

Notes:

Website:

Username: | Email:

Password:

Security Question 1:

Security Answer 1:

Security Question 2:

Security Answer 2:

Notes:

Website:

Username: | Email:

Password:

Security Question 1:

Security Answer 1:

Security Question 2:

Security Answer 2:

Notes:

Website:

Username: | Email:

Password:

Security Question 1:

Security Answer 1:

Security Question 2:

Security Answer 2:

Notes:

Website:

Username: Email:

Password:

Security Question 1:

Security Answer 1:

Security Question 2:

Security Answer 2:

Notes:

Website:

Username: Email:

Password:

Security Question 1:

Security Answer 1:

Security Question 2:

Security Answer 2:

Notes:

Website:

Username: Email:

Password:

Security Question 1:

Security Answer 1:

Security Question 2:

Security Answer 2:

Notes:

Website:

Username: Email:

Password:

Security Question 1:

Security Answer 1:

Security Question 2:

Security Answer 2:

Notes:

Website:

Username: Email:

Password:

Security Question 1:

Security Answer 1:

Security Question 2:

Security Answer 2:

Notes:

Website:

Username: Email:

Password:

Security Question 1:

Security Answer 1:

Security Question 2:

Security Answer 2:

Notes:

J

Website:

Username: Email:

Password:

Security Question 1:

Security Answer 1:

Security Question 2:

Security Answer 2:

Notes:

Website:

Username: Email:

Password:

Security Question 1:

Security Answer 1:

Security Question 2:

Security Answer 2:

Notes:

Website:

Username: Email:

Password:

Security Question 1:

Security Answer 1:

Security Question 2:

Security Answer 2:

Notes:

Website:

Username: Email:

Password:

Security Question 1:

Security Answer 1:

Security Question 2:

Security Answer 2:

Notes:

Website:

Username: Email:

Password:

Security Question 1:

Security Answer 1:

Security Question 2:

Security Answer 2:

Notes:

Website:

Username: Email:

Password:

Security Question 1:

Security Answer 1:

Security Question 2:

Security Answer 2:

Notes:

J

Website:

Username: Email:

Password:

Security Question 1:

Security Answer 1:

Security Question 2:

Security Answer 2:

Notes:

Website:

Username: Email:

Password:

Security Question 1:

Security Answer 1:

Security Question 2:

Security Answer 2:

Notes:

Website:

Username: Email:

Password:

Security Question 1:

Security Answer 1:

Security Question 2:

Security Answer 2:

Notes:

Website:

Username: Email:

Password:

Security Question 1:

Security Answer 1:

Security Question 2:

Security Answer 2:

Notes:

Website:

Username: Email:

Password:

Security Question 1:

Security Answer 1:

Security Question 2:

Security Answer 2:

Notes:

Website:

Username: Email:

Password:

Security Question 1:

Security Answer 1:

Security Question 2:

Security Answer 2:

Notes:

Website:

Username: Email:

Password:

Security Question 1:

Security Answer 1:

Security Question 2:

Security Answer 2:

Notes:

Website:

Username: Email:

Password:

Security Question 1:

Security Answer 1:

Security Question 2:

Security Answer 2:

Notes:

Website:

Username: Email:

Password:

Security Question 1:

Security Answer 1:

Security Question 2:

Security Answer 2:

Notes:

Website:

Username: Email:

Password:

Security Question 1:

Security Answer 1:

Security Question 2:

Security Answer 2:

Notes:

Website:

Username: Email:

Password:

Security Question 1:

Security Answer 1:

Security Question 2:

Security Answer 2:

Notes:

Website:

Username: Email:

Password:

Security Question 1:

Security Answer 1:

Security Question 2:

Security Answer 2:

Notes:

Website:

Username: Email:

Password:

Security Question 1:

Security Answer 1:

Security Question 2:

Security Answer 2:

Notes:

Website:

Username: Email:

Password:

Security Question 1:

Security Answer 1:

Security Question 2:

Security Answer 2:

Notes:

Website:

Username: Email:

Password:

Security Question 1:

Security Answer 1:

Security Question 2:

Security Answer 2:

Notes:

Website:

Username: Email:

Password:

Security Question 1:

Security Answer 1:

Security Question 2:

Security Answer 2:

Notes:

Website:

Username: Email:

Password:

Security Question 1:

Security Answer 1:

Security Question 2:

Security Answer 2:

Notes:

Website:

Username: Email:

Password:

Security Question 1:

Security Answer 1:

Security Question 2:

Security Answer 2:

Notes:

Website:

Username: Email:

Password:

Security Question 1:

Security Answer 1:

Security Question 2:

Security Answer 2:

Notes:

Website:

Username: Email:

Password:

Security Question 1:

Security Answer 1:

Security Question 2:

Security Answer 2:

Notes:

Website:

Username: Email:

Password:

Security Question 1:

Security Answer 1:

Security Question 2:

Security Answer 2:

Notes:

Website:

Username: Email:

Password:

Security Question 1:

Security Answer 1:

Security Question 2:

Security Answer 2:

Notes:

Website:

Username: Email:

Password:

Security Question 1:

Security Answer 1:

Security Question 2:

Security Answer 2:

Notes:

Website:

Username: Email:

Password:

Security Question 1:

Security Answer 1:

Security Question 2:

Security Answer 2:

Notes:

L

Website:

Username: Email:

Password:

Security Question 1:

Security Answer 1:

Security Question 2:

Security Answer 2:

Notes:

Website:

Username: Email:

Password:

Security Question 1:

Security Answer 1:

Security Question 2:

Security Answer 2:

Notes:

Website:

Username: Email:

Password:

Security Question 1:

Security Answer 1:

Security Question 2:

Security Answer 2:

Notes:

L

Website:

Username: Email:

Password:

Security Question 1:

Security Answer 1:

Security Question 2:

Security Answer 2:

Notes:

Website:

Username: Email:

Password:

Security Question 1:

Security Answer 1:

Security Question 2:

Security Answer 2:

Notes:

Website:

Username: Email:

Password:

Security Question 1:

Security Answer 1:

Security Question 2:

Security Answer 2:

Notes:

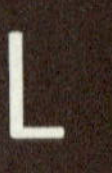

Website:

Username: Email:

Password:

Security Question 1:

Security Answer 1:

Security Question 2:

Security Answer 2:

Notes:

Website:

Username: Email:

Password:

Security Question 1:

Security Answer 1:

Security Question 2:

Security Answer 2:

Notes:

Website:

Username: Email:

Password:

Security Question 1:

Security Answer 1:

Security Question 2:

Security Answer 2:

Notes:

Website:

Username:

Email:

Password:

Security Question 1:

Security Answer 1:

Security Question 2:

Security Answer 2:

Notes:

Website:

Username:

Email:

Password:

Security Question 1:

Security Answer 1:

Security Question 2:

Security Answer 2:

Notes:

Website:

Username:

Email:

Password:

Security Question 1:

Security Answer 1:

Security Question 2:

Security Answer 2:

Notes:

L

Website:

Username: _______________ Email: _______________

Password: _______________

Security Question 1: _______________

Security Answer 1: _______________

Security Question 2: _______________

Security Answer 2: _______________

Notes: _______________

Website:

Username: _______________ Email: _______________

Password: _______________

Security Question 1: _______________

Security Answer 1: _______________

Security Question 2: _______________

Security Answer 2: _______________

Notes: _______________

Website:

Username: _______________ Email: _______________

Password: _______________

Security Question 1: _______________

Security Answer 1: _______________

Security Question 2: _______________

Security Answer 2: _______________

Notes: _______________

L

Website:

Username: Email:

Password:

Security Question 1:

Security Answer 1:

Security Question 2:

Security Answer 2:

Notes:

Website:

Username: Email:

Password:

Security Question 1:

Security Answer 1:

Security Question 2:

Security Answer 2:

Notes:

Website:

Username: Email:

Password:

Security Question 1:

Security Answer 1:

Security Question 2:

Security Answer 2:

Notes:

Website:

Username: Email:

Password:

Security Question 1:

Security Answer 1:

Security Question 2:

Security Answer 2:

Notes:

Website:

Username: Email:

Password:

Security Question 1:

Security Answer 1:

Security Question 2:

Security Answer 2:

Notes:

Website:

Username: Email:

Password:

Security Question 1:

Security Answer 1:

Security Question 2:

Security Answer 2:

Notes:

Website:

Username: Email:

Password:

Security Question 1:

Security Answer 1:

Security Question 2:

Security Answer 2:

Notes:

Website:

Username: Email:

Password:

Security Question 1:

Security Answer 1:

Security Question 2:

Security Answer 2:

Notes:

Website:

Username: Email:

Password:

Security Question 1:

Security Answer 1:

Security Question 2:

Security Answer 2:

Notes:

Website:

Username: Email:

Password:

Security Question 1:

Security Answer 1:

Security Question 2:

Security Answer 2:

Notes:

Website:

Username: Email:

Password:

Security Question 1:

Security Answer 1:

Security Question 2:

Security Answer 2:

Notes:

Website:

Username: Email:

Password:

Security Question 1:

Security Answer 1:

Security Question 2:

Security Answer 2:

Notes:

Website:

Username: Email:

Password:

Security Question 1:

Security Answer 1:

Security Question 2:

Security Answer 2:

Notes:

Website:

Username: Email:

Password:

Security Question 1:

Security Answer 1:

Security Question 2:

Security Answer 2:

Notes:

Website:

Username: Email:

Password:

Security Question 1:

Security Answer 1:

Security Question 2:

Security Answer 2:

Notes:

Website:

Username: _______________ Email: _______________

Password: _______________

Security Question 1: _______________

Security Answer 1: _______________

Security Question 2: _______________

Security Answer 2: _______________

Notes: _______________

Website:

Username: _______________ Email: _______________

Password: _______________

Security Question 1: _______________

Security Answer 1: _______________

Security Question 2: _______________

Security Answer 2: _______________

Notes: _______________

Website:

Username: _______________ Email: _______________

Password: _______________

Security Question 1: _______________

Security Answer 1: _______________

Security Question 2: _______________

Security Answer 2: _______________

Notes: _______________

Website:

Username: | Email:

Password:

Security Question 1:

Security Answer 1:

Security Question 2:

Security Answer 2:

Notes:

Website:

Username: | Email:

Password:

Security Question 1:

Security Answer 1:

Security Question 2:

Security Answer 2:

Notes:

Website:

Username: | Email:

Password:

Security Question 1:

Security Answer 1:

Security Question 2:

Security Answer 2:

Notes:

Website:

Username: Email:

Password:

Security Question 1:

Security Answer 1:

Security Question 2:

Security Answer 2:

Notes:

Website:

Username: Email:

Password:

Security Question 1:

Security Answer 1:

Security Question 2:

Security Answer 2:

Notes:

Website:

Username: Email:

Password:

Security Question 1:

Security Answer 1:

Security Question 2:

Security Answer 2:

Notes:

N

Website:

Username: Email:

Password:

Security Question 1:

Security Answer 1:

Security Question 2:

Security Answer 2:

Notes:

Website:

Username: Email:

Password:

Security Question 1:

Security Answer 1:

Security Question 2:

Security Answer 2:

Notes:

Website:

Username: Email:

Password:

Security Question 1:

Security Answer 1:

Security Question 2:

Security Answer 2:

Notes:

N

Website:

Username:	Email:

Password:

Security Question 1:

Security Answer 1:

Security Question 2:

Security Answer 2:

Notes:

Website:

Username:	Email:

Password:

Security Question 1:

Security Answer 1:

Security Question 2:

Security Answer 2:

Notes:

Website:

Username:	Email:

Password:

Security Question 1:

Security Answer 1:

Security Question 2:

Security Answer 2:

Notes:

Website:

Username: Email:

Password:

Security Question 1:

Security Answer 1:

Security Question 2:

Security Answer 2:

Notes:

Website:

Username: Email:

Password:

Security Question 1:

Security Answer 1:

Security Question 2:

Security Answer 2:

Notes:

Website:

Username: Email:

Password:

Security Question 1:

Security Answer 1:

Security Question 2:

Security Answer 2:

Notes:

Website:

Username: Email:

Password:

Security Question 1:

Security Answer 1:

Security Question 2:

Security Answer 2:

Notes:

Website:

Username: Email:

Password:

Security Question 1:

Security Answer 1:

Security Question 2:

Security Answer 2:

Notes:

Website:

Username: Email:

Password:

Security Question 1:

Security Answer 1:

Security Question 2:

Security Answer 2:

Notes:

N

Website:

Username: Email:

Password:

Security Question 1:

Security Answer 1:

Security Question 2:

Security Answer 2:

Notes:

Website:

Username: Email:

Password:

Security Question 1:

Security Answer 1:

Security Question 2:

Security Answer 2:

Notes:

Website:

Username: Email:

Password:

Security Question 1:

Security Answer 1:

Security Question 2:

Security Answer 2:

Notes:

Website:

Username: Email:

Password:

Security Question 1:

Security Answer 1:

Security Question 2:

Security Answer 2:

Notes:

Website:

Username: Email:

Password:

Security Question 1:

Security Answer 1:

Security Question 2:

Security Answer 2:

Notes:

Website:

Username: Email:

Password:

Security Question 1:

Security Answer 1:

Security Question 2:

Security Answer 2:

Notes:

O

Website:

Username: Email:

Password:

Security Question 1:

Security Answer 1:

Security Question 2:

Security Answer 2:

Notes:

Website:

Username: Email:

Password:

Security Question 1:

Security Answer 1:

Security Question 2:

Security Answer 2:

Notes:

Website:

Username: Email:

Password:

Security Question 1:

Security Answer 1:

Security Question 2:

Security Answer 2:

Notes:

O

Website:

Username: Email:

Password:

Security Question 1:

Security Answer 1:

Security Question 2:

Security Answer 2:

Notes:

Website:

Username: Email:

Password:

Security Question 1:

Security Answer 1:

Security Question 2:

Security Answer 2:

Notes:

Website:

Username: Email:

Password:

Security Question 1:

Security Answer 1:

Security Question 2:

Security Answer 2:

Notes:

Website:

Username: Email:

Password:

Security Question 1:

Security Answer 1:

Security Question 2:

Security Answer 2:

Notes:

Website:

Username: Email:

Password:

Security Question 1:

Security Answer 1:

Security Question 2:

Security Answer 2:

Notes:

Website:

Username: Email:

Password:

Security Question 1:

Security Answer 1:

Security Question 2:

Security Answer 2:

Notes:

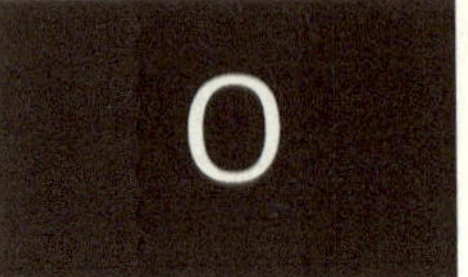

Website:

Username: Email:

Password:

Security Question 1:

Security Answer 1:

Security Question 2:

Security Answer 2:

Notes:

Website:

Username: Email:

Password:

Security Question 1:

Security Answer 1:

Security Question 2:

Security Answer 2:

Notes:

Website:

Username: Email:

Password:

Security Question 1:

Security Answer 1:

Security Question 2:

Security Answer 2:

Notes:

Website:

Username: Email:

Password:

Security Question 1:

Security Answer 1:

Security Question 2:

Security Answer 2:

Notes:

Website:

Username: Email:

Password:

Security Question 1:

Security Answer 1:

Security Question 2:

Security Answer 2:

Notes:

Website:

Username: Email:

Password:

Security Question 1:

Security Answer 1:

Security Question 2:

Security Answer 2:

Notes:

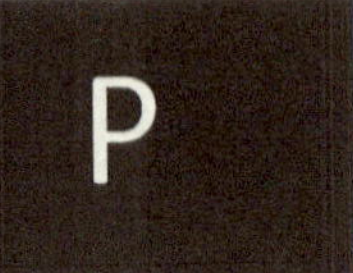

Website:

Username: Email:

Password:

Security Question 1:

Security Answer 1:

Security Question 2:

Security Answer 2:

Notes:

Website:

Username: Email:

Password:

Security Question 1:

Security Answer 1:

Security Question 2:

Security Answer 2:

Notes:

Website:

Username: Email:

Password:

Security Question 1:

Security Answer 1:

Security Question 2:

Security Answer 2:

Notes:

P

Website:

Username: Email:

Password:

Security Question 1:

Security Answer 1:

Security Question 2:

Security Answer 2:

Notes:

Website:

Username: Email:

Password:

Security Question 1:

Security Answer 1:

Security Question 2:

Security Answer 2:

Notes:

Website:

Username: Email:

Password:

Security Question 1:

Security Answer 1:

Security Question 2:

Security Answer 2:

Notes:

P

Website:

Username: Email:

Password:

Security Question 1:

Security Answer 1:

Security Question 2:

Security Answer 2:

Notes:

Website:

Username: Email:

Password:

Security Question 1:

Security Answer 1:

Security Question 2:

Security Answer 2:

Notes:

Website:

Username: Email:

Password:

Security Question 1:

Security Answer 1:

Security Question 2:

Security Answer 2:

Notes:

Website:

Username: Email:

Password:

Security Question 1:

Security Answer 1:

Security Question 2:

Security Answer 2:

Notes:

Website:

Username: Email:

Password:

Security Question 1:

Security Answer 1:

Security Question 2:

Security Answer 2:

Notes:

Website:

Username: Email:

Password:

Security Question 1:

Security Answer 1:

Security Question 2:

Security Answer 2:

Notes:

Website:

Username: Email:

Password:

Security Question 1:

Security Answer 1:

Security Question 2:

Security Answer 2:

Notes:

Website:

Username: Email:

Password:

Security Question 1:

Security Answer 1:

Security Question 2:

Security Answer 2:

Notes:

Website:

Username: Email:

Password:

Security Question 1:

Security Answer 1:

Security Question 2:

Security Answer 2:

Notes:

Website:	
Username:	Email:
Password:	
Security Question 1:	
Security Answer 1:	
Security Question 2:	
Security Answer 2:	
Notes:	

Website:	
Username:	Email:
Password:	
Security Question 1:	
Security Answer 1:	
Security Question 2:	
Security Answer 2:	
Notes:	

Website:	
Username:	Email:
Password:	
Security Question 1:	
Security Answer 1:	
Security Question 2:	
Security Answer 2:	
Notes:	

Website:

Username: Email:

Password:

Security Question 1:

Security Answer 1:

Security Question 2:

Security Answer 2:

Notes:

Website:

Username: Email:

Password:

Security Question 1:

Security Answer 1:

Security Question 2:

Security Answer 2:

Notes:

Website:

Username: Email:

Password:

Security Question 1:

Security Answer 1:

Security Question 2:

Security Answer 2:

Notes:

Q

Website:

Username: Email:

Password:

Security Question 1:

Security Answer 1:

Security Question 2:

Security Answer 2:

Notes:

Website:

Username: Email:

Password:

Security Question 1:

Security Answer 1:

Security Question 2:

Security Answer 2:

Notes:

Website:

Username: Email:

Password:

Security Question 1:

Security Answer 1:

Security Question 2:

Security Answer 2:

Notes:

Q

Website:

Username: Email:

Password:

Security Question 1:

Security Answer 1:

Security Question 2:

Security Answer 2:

Notes:

Website:

Username: Email:

Password:

Security Question 1:

Security Answer 1:

Security Question 2:

Security Answer 2:

Notes:

Website:

Username: Email:

Password:

Security Question 1:

Security Answer 1:

Security Question 2:

Security Answer 2:

Notes:

Q

Website:

Username: Email:

Password:

Security Question 1:

Security Answer 1:

Security Question 2:

Security Answer 2:

Notes:

Website:

Username: Email:

Password:

Security Question 1:

Security Answer 1:

Security Question 2:

Security Answer 2:

Notes:

Website:

Username: Email:

Password:

Security Question 1:

Security Answer 1:

Security Question 2:

Security Answer 2:

Notes:

Website:

Username: Email:

Password:

Security Question 1:

Security Answer 1:

Security Question 2:

Security Answer 2:

Notes:

Website:

Username: Email:

Password:

Security Question 1:

Security Answer 1:

Security Question 2:

Security Answer 2:

Notes:

Website:

Username: Email:

Password:

Security Question 1:

Security Answer 1:

Security Question 2:

Security Answer 2:

Notes:

Website:

Username: Email:

Password:

Security Question 1:

Security Answer 1:

Security Question 2:

Security Answer 2:

Notes:

Website:

Username: Email:

Password:

Security Question 1:

Security Answer 1:

Security Question 2:

Security Answer 2:

Notes:

Website:

Username: Email:

Password:

Security Question 1:

Security Answer 1:

Security Question 2:

Security Answer 2:

Notes:

R

Website:

Username: Email:

Password:

Security Question 1:

Security Answer 1:

Security Question 2:

Security Answer 2:

Notes:

Website:

Username: Email:

Password:

Security Question 1:

Security Answer 1:

Security Question 2:

Security Answer 2:

Notes:

Website:

Username: Email:

Password:

Security Question 1:

Security Answer 1:

Security Question 2:

Security Answer 2:

Notes:

Website:

Username: Email:

Password:

Security Question 1:

Security Answer 1:

Security Question 2:

Security Answer 2:

Notes:

Website:

Username: Email:

Password:

Security Question 1:

Security Answer 1:

Security Question 2:

Security Answer 2:

Notes:

Website:

Username: Email:

Password:

Security Question 1:

Security Answer 1:

Security Question 2:

Security Answer 2:

Notes:

Website:

Username: Email:

Password:

Security Question 1:

Security Answer 1:

Security Question 2:

Security Answer 2:

Notes:

Website:

Username: Email:

Password:

Security Question 1:

Security Answer 1:

Security Question 2:

Security Answer 2:

Notes:

Website:

Username: Email:

Password:

Security Question 1:

Security Answer 1:

Security Question 2:

Security Answer 2:

Notes:

Website:

Username: Email:

Password:

Security Question 1:

Security Answer 1:

Security Question 2:

Security Answer 2:

Notes:

Website:

Username: Email:

Password:

Security Question 1:

Security Answer 1:

Security Question 2:

Security Answer 2:

Notes:

Website:

Username: Email:

Password:

Security Question 1:

Security Answer 1:

Security Question 2:

Security Answer 2:

Notes:

Website:

Username: Email:

Password:

Security Question 1:

Security Answer 1:

Security Question 2:

Security Answer 2:

Notes:

Website:

Username: Email:

Password:

Security Question 1:

Security Answer 1:

Security Question 2:

Security Answer 2:

Notes:

Website:

Username: Email:

Password:

Security Question 1:

Security Answer 1:

Security Question 2:

Security Answer 2:

Notes:

Website:

Username: Email:

Password:

Security Question 1:

Security Answer 1:

Security Question 2:

Security Answer 2:

Notes:

Website:

Username: Email:

Password:

Security Question 1:

Security Answer 1:

Security Question 2:

Security Answer 2:

Notes:

Website:

Username: Email:

Password:

Security Question 1:

Security Answer 1:

Security Question 2:

Security Answer 2:

Notes:

S

Website:

Username: Email:

Password:

Security Question 1:

Security Answer 1:

Security Question 2:

Security Answer 2:

Notes:

Website:

Username: Email:

Password:

Security Question 1:

Security Answer 1:

Security Question 2:

Security Answer 2:

Notes:

Website:

Username: Email:

Password:

Security Question 1:

Security Answer 1:

Security Question 2:

Security Answer 2:

Notes:

S

Website:

Username: | Email:

Password:

Security Question 1:

Security Answer 1:

Security Question 2:

Security Answer 2:

Notes:

Website:

Username: | Email:

Password:

Security Question 1:

Security Answer 1:

Security Question 2:

Security Answer 2:

Notes:

Website:

Username: | Email:

Password:

Security Question 1:

Security Answer 1:

Security Question 2:

Security Answer 2:

Notes:

Website:

Username: Email:

Password:

Security Question 1:

Security Answer 1:

Security Question 2:

Security Answer 2:

Notes:

Website:

Username: Email:

Password:

Security Question 1:

Security Answer 1:

Security Question 2:

Security Answer 2:

Notes:

Website:

Username: Email:

Password:

Security Question 1:

Security Answer 1:

Security Question 2:

Security Answer 2:

Notes:

S

Website:

Username: Email:

Password:

Security Question 1:

Security Answer 1:

Security Question 2:

Security Answer 2:

Notes:

Website:

Username: Email:

Password:

Security Question 1:

Security Answer 1:

Security Question 2:

Security Answer 2:

Notes:

Website:

Username: Email:

Password:

Security Question 1:

Security Answer 1:

Security Question 2:

Security Answer 2:

Notes:

S

Website:

Username: Email:

Password:

Security Question 1:

Security Answer 1:

Security Question 2:

Security Answer 2:

Notes:

Website:

Username: Email:

Password:

Security Question 1:

Security Answer 1:

Security Question 2:

Security Answer 2:

Notes:

Website:

Username: Email:

Password:

Security Question 1:

Security Answer 1:

Security Question 2:

Security Answer 2:

Notes:

Website:

Username: Email:

Password:

Security Question 1:

Security Answer 1:

Security Question 2:

Security Answer 2:

Notes:

Website:

Username: Email:

Password:

Security Question 1:

Security Answer 1:

Security Question 2:

Security Answer 2:

Notes:

Website:

Username: Email:

Password:

Security Question 1:

Security Answer 1:

Security Question 2:

Security Answer 2:

Notes:

Website:

Username: Email:

Password:

Security Question 1:

Security Answer 1:

Security Question 2:

Security Answer 2:

Notes:

Website:

Username: Email:

Password:

Security Question 1:

Security Answer 1:

Security Question 2:

Security Answer 2:

Notes:

Website:

Username: Email:

Password:

Security Question 1:

Security Answer 1:

Security Question 2:

Security Answer 2:

Notes:

T

Website:

Username: Email:

Password:

Security Question 1:

Security Answer 1:

Security Question 2:

Security Answer 2:

Notes:

Website:

Username: Email:

Password:

Security Question 1:

Security Answer 1:

Security Question 2:

Security Answer 2:

Notes:

Website:

Username: Email:

Password:

Security Question 1:

Security Answer 1:

Security Question 2:

Security Answer 2:

Notes:

T

Website:

Username: Email:

Password:

Security Question 1:

Security Answer 1:

Security Question 2:

Security Answer 2:

Notes:

Website:

Username: Email:

Password:

Security Question 1:

Security Answer 1:

Security Question 2:

Security Answer 2:

Notes:

Website:

Username: Email:

Password:

Security Question 1:

Security Answer 1:

Security Question 2:

Security Answer 2:

Notes:

T

Website:

Username: | Email:

Password:

Security Question 1:

Security Answer 1:

Security Question 2:

Security Answer 2:

Notes:

Website:

Username: | Email:

Password:

Security Question 1:

Security Answer 1:

Security Question 2:

Security Answer 2:

Notes:

Website:

Username: | Email:

Password:

Security Question 1:

Security Answer 1:

Security Question 2:

Security Answer 2:

Notes:

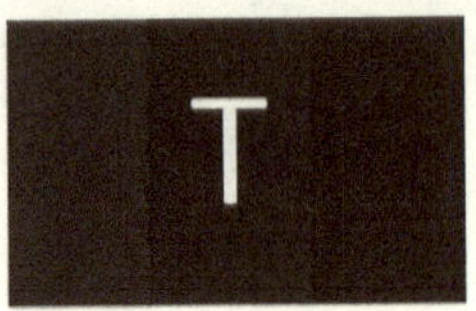

Website:

Username: Email:

Password:

Security Question 1:

Security Answer 1:

Security Question 2:

Security Answer 2:

Notes:

Website:

Username: Email:

Password:

Security Question 1:

Security Answer 1:

Security Question 2:

Security Answer 2:

Notes:

Website:

Username: Email:

Password:

Security Question 1:

Security Answer 1:

Security Question 2:

Security Answer 2:

Notes:

Website:

Username: Email:

Password:

Security Question 1:

Security Answer 1:

Security Question 2:

Security Answer 2:

Notes:

Website:

Username: Email:

Password:

Security Question 1:

Security Answer 1:

Security Question 2:

Security Answer 2:

Notes:

Website:

Username: Email:

Password:

Security Question 1:

Security Answer 1:

Security Question 2:

Security Answer 2:

Notes:

Website:

Username: Email:

Password:

Security Question 1:

Security Answer 1:

Security Question 2:

Security Answer 2:

Notes:

Website:

Username: Email:

Password:

Security Question 1:

Security Answer 1:

Security Question 2:

Security Answer 2:

Notes:

Website:

Username: Email:

Password:

Security Question 1:

Security Answer 1:

Security Question 2:

Security Answer 2:

Notes:

Website:

Username: Email:

Password:

Security Question 1:

Security Answer 1:

Security Question 2:

Security Answer 2:

Notes:

Website:

Username: Email:

Password:

Security Question 1:

Security Answer 1:

Security Question 2:

Security Answer 2:

Notes:

Website:

Username: Email:

Password:

Security Question 1:

Security Answer 1:

Security Question 2:

Security Answer 2:

Notes:

Website:

Username: Email:

Password:

Security Question 1:

Security Answer 1:

Security Question 2:

Security Answer 2:

Notes:

Website:

Username: Email:

Password:

Security Question 1:

Security Answer 1:

Security Question 2:

Security Answer 2:

Notes:

Website:

Username: Email:

Password:

Security Question 1:

Security Answer 1:

Security Question 2:

Security Answer 2:

Notes:

Website:

Username: Email:

Password:

Security Question 1:

Security Answer 1:

Security Question 2:

Security Answer 2:

Notes:

Website:

Username: Email:

Password:

Security Question 1:

Security Answer 1:

Security Question 2:

Security Answer 2:

Notes:

Website:

Username: Email:

Password:

Security Question 1:

Security Answer 1:

Security Question 2:

Security Answer 2:

Notes:

Website:

Username: Email:

Password:

Security Question 1:

Security Answer 1:

Security Question 2:

Security Answer 2:

Notes:

Website:

Username: Email:

Password:

Security Question 1:

Security Answer 1:

Security Question 2:

Security Answer 2:

Notes:

Website:

Username: Email:

Password:

Security Question 1:

Security Answer 1:

Security Question 2:

Security Answer 2:

Notes:

Website:

Username: Email:

Password:

Security Question 1:

Security Answer 1:

Security Question 2:

Security Answer 2:

Notes:

Website:

Username: Email:

Password:

Security Question 1:

Security Answer 1:

Security Question 2:

Security Answer 2:

Notes:

Website:

Username: Email:

Password:

Security Question 1:

Security Answer 1:

Security Question 2:

Security Answer 2:

Notes:

Website:

Username: Email:

Password:

Security Question 1:

Security Answer 1:

Security Question 2:

Security Answer 2:

Notes:

Website:

Username: Email:

Password:

Security Question 1:

Security Answer 1:

Security Question 2:

Security Answer 2:

Notes:

Website:

Username: Email:

Password:

Security Question 1:

Security Answer 1:

Security Question 2:

Security Answer 2:

Notes:

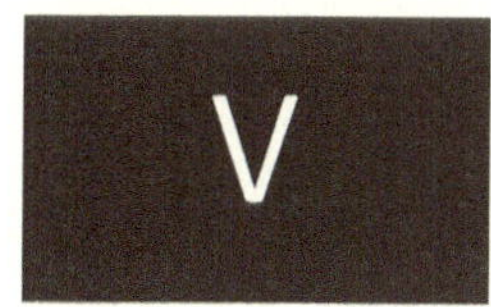

Website:

Username: Email:

Password:

Security Question 1:

Security Answer 1:

Security Question 2:

Security Answer 2:

Notes:

Website:

Username: Email:

Password:

Security Question 1:

Security Answer 1:

Security Question 2:

Security Answer 2:

Notes:

Website:

Username: Email:

Password:

Security Question 1:

Security Answer 1:

Security Question 2:

Security Answer 2:

Notes:

Website:

Username: Email:

Password:

Security Question 1:

Security Answer 1:

Security Question 2:

Security Answer 2:

Notes:

Website:

Username: Email:

Password:

Security Question 1:

Security Answer 1:

Security Question 2:

Security Answer 2:

Notes:

Website:

Username: Email:

Password:

Security Question 1:

Security Answer 1:

Security Question 2:

Security Answer 2:

Notes:

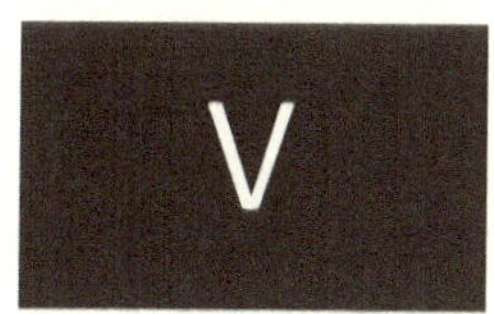

Website:

Username: Email:

Password:

Security Question 1:

Security Answer 1:

Security Question 2:

Security Answer 2:

Notes:

Website:

Username: Email:

Password:

Security Question 1:

Security Answer 1:

Security Question 2:

Security Answer 2:

Notes:

Website:

Username: Email:

Password:

Security Question 1:

Security Answer 1:

Security Question 2:

Security Answer 2:

Notes:

Website:

Username: Email:

Password:

Security Question 1:

Security Answer 1:

Security Question 2:

Security Answer 2:

Notes:

Website:

Username: Email:

Password:

Security Question 1:

Security Answer 1:

Security Question 2:

Security Answer 2:

Notes:

Website:

Username: Email:

Password:

Security Question 1:

Security Answer 1:

Security Question 2:

Security Answer 2:

Notes:

Website:

Username: Email:

Password:

Security Question 1:

Security Answer 1:

Security Question 2:

Security Answer 2:

Notes:

Website:

Username: Email:

Password:

Security Question 1:

Security Answer 1:

Security Question 2:

Security Answer 2:

Notes:

Website:

Username: Email:

Password:

Security Question 1:

Security Answer 1:

Security Question 2:

Security Answer 2:

Notes:

Website:

Username: Email:

Password:

Security Question 1:

Security Answer 1:

Security Question 2:

Security Answer 2:

Notes:

Website:

Username: Email:

Password:

Security Question 1:

Security Answer 1:

Security Question 2:

Security Answer 2:

Notes:

Website:

Username: Email:

Password:

Security Question 1:

Security Answer 1:

Security Question 2:

Security Answer 2:

Notes:

Website:

Username: Email:

Password:

Security Question 1:

Security Answer 1:

Security Question 2:

Security Answer 2:

Notes:

Website:

Username: Email:

Password:

Security Question 1:

Security Answer 1:

Security Question 2:

Security Answer 2:

Notes:

Website:

Username: Email:

Password:

Security Question 1:

Security Answer 1:

Security Question 2:

Security Answer 2:

Notes:

Website:

Username: Email:

Password:

Security Question 1:

Security Answer 1:

Security Question 2:

Security Answer 2:

Notes:

Website:

Username: Email:

Password:

Security Question 1:

Security Answer 1:

Security Question 2:

Security Answer 2:

Notes:

Website:

Username: Email:

Password:

Security Question 1:

Security Answer 1:

Security Question 2:

Security Answer 2:

Notes:

Website:

Username: Email:

Password:

Security Question 1:

Security Answer 1:

Security Question 2:

Security Answer 2:

Notes:

Website:

Username: Email:

Password:

Security Question 1:

Security Answer 1:

Security Question 2:

Security Answer 2:

Notes:

Website:

Username: Email:

Password:

Security Question 1:

Security Answer 1:

Security Question 2:

Security Answer 2:

Notes:

Website:

Username: Email:

Password:

Security Question 1:

Security Answer 1:

Security Question 2:

Security Answer 2:

Notes:

Website:

Username: Email:

Password:

Security Question 1:

Security Answer 1:

Security Question 2:

Security Answer 2:

Notes:

Website:

Username: Email:

Password:

Security Question 1:

Security Answer 1:

Security Question 2:

Security Answer 2:

Notes:

Website:

Username: Email:

Password:

Security Question 1:

Security Answer 1:

Security Question 2:

Security Answer 2:

Notes:

Website:

Username: Email:

Password:

Security Question 1:

Security Answer 1:

Security Question 2:

Security Answer 2:

Notes:

Website:

Username: Email:

Password:

Security Question 1:

Security Answer 1:

Security Question 2:

Security Answer 2:

Notes:

Website:

Username:	Email:

Password:

Security Question 1:

Security Answer 1:

Security Question 2:

Security Answer 2:

Notes:

Website:

Username:	Email:

Password:

Security Question 1:

Security Answer 1:

Security Question 2:

Security Answer 2:

Notes:

Website:

Username:	Email:

Password:

Security Question 1:

Security Answer 1:

Security Question 2:

Security Answer 2:

Notes:

Website:

Username: Email:

Password:

Security Question 1:

Security Answer 1:

Security Question 2:

Security Answer 2:

Notes:

Website:

Username: Email:

Password:

Security Question 1:

Security Answer 1:

Security Question 2:

Security Answer 2:

Notes:

Website:

Username: Email:

Password:

Security Question 1:

Security Answer 1:

Security Question 2:

Security Answer 2:

Notes:

Website:

Username: Email:

Password:

Security Question 1:

Security Answer 1:

Security Question 2:

Security Answer 2:

Notes:

Website:

Username: Email:

Password:

Security Question 1:

Security Answer 1:

Security Question 2:

Security Answer 2:

Notes:

Website:

Username: Email:

Password:

Security Question 1:

Security Answer 1:

Security Question 2:

Security Answer 2:

Notes:

Website:

Username: | Email:

Password:

Security Question 1:

Security Answer 1:

Security Question 2:

Security Answer 2:

Notes:

Website:

Username: | Email:

Password:

Security Question 1:

Security Answer 1:

Security Question 2:

Security Answer 2:

Notes:

Website:

Username: | Email:

Password:

Security Question 1:

Security Answer 1:

Security Question 2:

Security Answer 2:

Notes:

Website:

Username: | Email:

Password:

Security Question 1:

Security Answer 1:

Security Question 2:

Security Answer 2:

Notes:

Website:

Username: | Email:

Password:

Security Question 1:

Security Answer 1:

Security Question 2:

Security Answer 2:

Notes:

Website:

Username: | Email:

Password:

Security Question 1:

Security Answer 1:

Security Question 2:

Security Answer 2:

Notes:

Website:

Username: ___________ Email: ___________

Password: ___________

Security Question 1: ___________

Security Answer 1: ___________

Security Question 2: ___________

Security Answer 2: ___________

Notes: ___________

Website:

Username: ___________ Email: ___________

Password: ___________

Security Question 1: ___________

Security Answer 1: ___________

Security Question 2: ___________

Security Answer 2: ___________

Notes: ___________

Website:

Username: ___________ Email: ___________

Password: ___________

Security Question 1: ___________

Security Answer 1: ___________

Security Question 2: ___________

Security Answer 2: ___________

Notes: ___________

Website:

Username: Email:

Password:

Security Question 1:

Security Answer 1:

Security Question 2:

Security Answer 2:

Notes:

Website:

Username: Email:

Password:

Security Question 1:

Security Answer 1:

Security Question 2:

Security Answer 2:

Notes:

Website:

Username: Email:

Password:

Security Question 1:

Security Answer 1:

Security Question 2:

Security Answer 2:

Notes:

Username: Email:

Password:

Security Question 1:

Security Answer 1:

Security Question 2:

Security Answer 2:

Notes:

Website:

Username: Email:

Password:

Security Question 1:

Security Answer 1:

Security Question 2:

Security Answer 2:

Notes:

Website:

Username: Email:

Password:

Security Question 1:

Security Answer 1:

Security Question 2:

Security Answer 2:

Notes:

Website:

Username: Email:

Password:

Security Question 1:

Security Answer 1:

Security Question 2:

Security Answer 2:

Notes:

Website:

Username: Email:

Password:

Security Question 1:

Security Answer 1:

Security Question 2:

Security Answer 2:

Notes:

Website:

Username: Email:

Password:

Security Question 1:

Security Answer 1:

Security Question 2:

Security Answer 2:

Notes:

Website:

Username: Email:

Password:

Security Question 1:

Security Answer 1:

Security Question 2:

Security Answer 2:

Notes:

Website:

Username: Email:

Password:

Security Question 1:

Security Answer 1:

Security Question 2:

Security Answer 2:

Notes:

Website:

Username: Email:

Password:

Security Question 1:

Security Answer 1:

Security Question 2:

Security Answer 2:

Notes:

Y

Website:

Username: Email:

Password:

Security Question 1:

Security Answer 1:

Security Question 2:

Security Answer 2:

Notes:

Website:

Username: Email:

Password:

Security Question 1:

Security Answer 1:

Security Question 2:

Security Answer 2:

Notes:

Website:

Username: Email:

Password:

Security Question 1:

Security Answer 1:

Security Question 2:

Security Answer 2:

Notes:

Website:

Username: Email:

Password:

Security Question 1:

Security Answer 1:

Security Question 2:

Security Answer 2:

Notes:

Website:

Username: Email:

Password:

Security Question 1:

Security Answer 1:

Security Question 2:

Security Answer 2:

Notes:

Website:

Username: Email:

Password:

Security Question 1:

Security Answer 1:

Security Question 2:

Security Answer 2:

Notes:

Z

Website:

Username: Email:

Password:

Security Question 1:

Security Answer 1:

Security Question 2:

Security Answer 2:

Notes:

Website:

Username: Email:

Password:

Security Question 1:

Security Answer 1:

Security Question 2:

Security Answer 2:

Notes:

Website:

Username: Email:

Password:

Security Question 1:

Security Answer 1:

Security Question 2:

Security Answer 2:

Notes:

Z

Website:

Username: Email:

Password:

Security Question 1:

Security Answer 1:

Security Question 2:

Security Answer 2:

Notes:

Website:

Username: Email:

Password:

Security Question 1:

Security Answer 1:

Security Question 2:

Security Answer 2:

Notes:

Website:

Username: Email:

Password:

Security Question 1:

Security Answer 1:

Security Question 2:

Security Answer 2:

Notes:

Z

Username: Email:

Password:

Security Question 1:

Security Answer 1:

Security Question 2:

Security Answer 2:

Notes:

Username: Email:

Password:

Security Question 1:

Security Answer 1:

Security Question 2:

Security Answer 2:

Notes:

Username: Email:

Password:

Security Question 1:

Security Answer 1:

Security Question 2:

Security Answer 2:

Notes:

Z

Website:

Username: Email:

Password:

Security Question 1:

Security Answer 1:

Security Question 2:

Security Answer 2:

Notes:

Website:

Username: Email:

Password:

Security Question 1:

Security Answer 1:

Security Question 2:

Security Answer 2:

Notes:

Website:

Username: Email:

Password:

Security Question 1:

Security Answer 1:

Security Question 2:

Security Answer 2:

Notes:

Z

Website:

Username: Email:

Password:

Security Question 1:

Security Answer 1:

Security Question 2:

Security Answer 2:

Notes:

Website:

Username: Email:

Password:

Security Question 1:

Security Answer 1:

Security Question 2:

Security Answer 2:

Notes:

Website:

Username: Email:

Password:

Security Question 1:

Security Answer 1:

Security Question 2:

Security Answer 2:

Notes:

Website:

Username: | Email:

Password:

Security Question 1:

Security Answer 1:

Security Question 2:

Security Answer 2:

Notes:

Website:

Username: | Email:

Password:

Security Question 1:

Security Answer 1:

Security Question 2:

Security Answer 2:

Notes:

Website:

Username: | Email:

Password:

Security Question 1:

Security Answer 1:

Security Question 2:

Security Answer 2:

Notes: